FEELING THE SHOULDER OF THE LION

FEELING
THE SHOULDER
OF THE LION

Selected Poetry and Teaching Stories
from the *Mathnawi*

Jelaluddin Rumi

Versions by Coleman Barks

THRESHOLD BOOKS

Threshold Books is committed to publishing books of spiritual significance with high literary quality. All Threshold books have sewn bindings, and are printed on acid-free paper.

We will be happy to send you a catalog.
Threshold Books, RD 4, Box 600, Putney, Vermont 05346

ISBN 0-939660-38-5
Library of Congress Catalog Card Number

Library of Congress Cataloging-in-Publication Data:
        Jalal al-Din al-Rumi, Maulana, 1207-1273.
        (Masnavi. English. Selections)
        Feeling The Shoulder of the Lion:
        selections from the Mathnawi /
        Jelaluddin Rumi ; versions by Coleman Barks.

        ISBN 0-939660-38-5

        1. Sufi poetry, Persian–Translation into English.
        I. Barks, Coleman II. Title.
        PK6481.M8E52 1991 891'.5511–dc20 91-4749

Contents

The Lion

MUCH of Rumi's poetry circles about the mystery of surrender. One aspect of that is a forcefulness. It might be called discipline, or clarity, or integrity. Certain images occur in this area of soul-growth. When Rumi talks about fasting, he often brings in the image of a lion:

> A beautiful meal looks delicious.
> Then one night passes, and the food passes
> through you, becoming repellent filth.
>
> Eat love-food.
> Suckle the toes of a Lion...
> > *Like This*

The *power* of the appetites is in the lion, the power to control them, or indulge them. Lion-energy doesn't discriminate between the two. The lion is also associated with the sun. The lion wants *more light*. Sometimes that means fasting, sometimes feasting. The spirit lion is the dawn presence, the one who calls out, announcing the next.

D.H. Lawrence describes a beast that he identifies with St. Mark as

> The lion of the spirit.
>
> The proud lion stalks abroad alone,
> And roars to announce himself to the wolves....
> > D.H Lawrence, *Complete Poems*

This is not a passive animal. This is not the part of the self that loves bewilderment and melting songs and drunken merging. This is the energy of ornery independence. The lion has dignity. His family group is called a pride. When Buddha returned to his students after the forty-nine day bodhi tree fast, he said, "Have I ever spoken to you like this? This is the roar of the lion!"

Nietzsche's Zarathustra describes the three stages of psychic metamorphosis in terms of a camel, a lion, and a child. The camel represents the devotee stage, when one carries burdens and kneels to a teacher and a teaching. The lion brings in that which does not imitate.

> In the loneliest desert the second metamorphosis occurs: The spirit here becomes a lion; it wants to capture freedom and be lord in its own desert. It seeks here its ultimate lord: it will be an enemy to him and to its ultimate God, it will struggle for victory with the great dragon. What is the great dragon which the spirit no longer wants to call lord and God? The great dragon is called "Thou Shalt." But the spirit of the lion says, "I Will!"
>
> Nietzsche, *Thus Spoke Zarathustra*

The lion says *no* to any dutiful carrying-on, or comfortable inertias. The spirit lion leads out of marginal, dependent existence into the danger and blankness of the desert. That's the lion's freedom. I associate the lion with Moses and Sophocles, with Abdul Jabbar Niffari, Padmasambhava, and Francis of Assisi, with King Lear, Goethe, Blake, and Keats, with D.H.Lawrence and Robinson Jeffers, with Mark Twain and Gary Snyder, with my friend Ed Hicks in Troy, Alabama, and with my son Benjamin. I feel the lion waking in me when I clear the decks, when I say *no*, and wait for some vastness to enter.

But there are gentle and great-hearted qualities to this stage of psychic evolution too. (See "Why the Prophets Are Human.") The lion leads to the child by expanding the horizon. In alchemy the lion is an intermediate transformational symbol. The green lion of raw matter gives birth to the sun by disgorging it with much blood. Shams, Rumi's teacher, is associated throughout the poetry with the spiritual sun, and with the lion. I don't mean to imply that there's an occult network of meanings that should be fussed over and mapped. Rumi uses the image of the lion in many different ways. In one poem it represents time itself (see "The Prophet's Vision"), but in most instances the lion is the point of necessity that comes at a certain moment, the fierce intensity that destroys ego-imprisonment, and opens one out into light and another field of being. Nietzsche's sequence is important. One doesn't move directly from camel to child, from devotee to new consciousness. Lion-energy is the bridge.

There are political aspects to the lion too. He roars. He speaks strong language and wants, above all else, for the truth to come out and be seen. When the lion enters, the revolution begins. Lion-energy and warrior-energy are close. In sufi stories sometimes a great eccentric teacher will be riding a lion. (See "Sheikh Kharraqani and His Wretched Wife" in *This Longing*.) Shams was associated with this animal, and he was completely his own man. Whenever students would begin to gather around him in a dependent relationship, he would excuse himself and vanish. He was called "Parinda," the winged one. Lions often have mythic wings. They look right with wings. They need them to flee the company of hypocrites and imitators. Lions carry no baggage. Each lion is his own path, and he wants everyone to take total responsibility for himself or herself. The lion in a human being is almost without cowardice, and he doesn't long for, or expect, protection. The lion is a knight out in the wilderness by himself. He has a *collectedness* in him that commands, even though he may be alone against an entire town. Of Ali it was said,

> You are alone,
> and yet you are the whole community.
> One and a hundred thousand.
> *Mathnawi*, I, 3875

In Islam, Ali is spoken of as God's Lion. His is the politics, and religion, of dignity, even more than love. You may have heard the famous story of Ali in battle ("Ali in Battle"). The calligraphy on the front of this book represents him.

Ali and the lion have been closely connected with the sufis and with esoteric secrets which can't be told. Ali was instructed in some truths by Muhammed, and was afterwards asked by another close friend of the Prophet, who was not initiated into those matters, what he had been told. "If I were to tell you, you would want to cut off my head."

To the spirit lion, devotion and ecstatic fullness are *not enough*. He wants the hard, clean threshing floor of emptiness where, in Nietzsche's terms, the child can create a fresh world. Or maybe Nietzsche is too categorical, and the stages of human development are more organic, each being brought along inside the other: the camel in the lion and both within the child.

If the lion's solitude doesn't have a core of devotion, it's hollow. If the lion hasn't bowed all the way down to a teacher, he turns mean. If the child hasn't the various strengths of the patient camel and the fearless lion, his joy is vague and uncreative. These are my speculations on Nietzsche's speculations.

But the chief lion attribute is his authority. It is an authority over himself, and it is also an authority that comes from living close to a deep sense of self that he will not betray. I remember seeing in the old Atlanta zoo a lion who stood in the middle of his cage all afternoon and moaned out a huge hollow protest. It was so powerful and clear that no one could bear to stay in that part of the building. Lions cannot live in cages, or be told what to do. Being a lion is not *fitting in*. He does not refer to group behavior, only to that which he generates and validates from within.

But lion-ness–whether trapped by civilization or wild, and however much it may be needed–is not Rumi's point. "Lion strength weakens to nothing." Human beings, be they camel or lion or child or gazelle or donkey, are here to *remember* that they're in *borrowed clothes*. All this magical body-finery is on loan, like stained glass, while it's letting sunlight through:

> "The crime is
> that they put on borrowed robes
> and pretended that they were theirs...."

The earth-colored glass
makes everything seem diverse,
but that glass eventually shatters.

Your lamp was lit from another lamp.
All God wants is your gratitude for that.

Lend, is the divine command.
Make God a loan from your existence....
"The Gazelle"

I hear the lion's roar in Rumi, but he certainly didn't stop with that thunderous *no* to what blocks light, to easy answers and the need to belong. He moved on out into an enormous open, into the creative *yes* of the child, and beyond. That joy is felt under all the words, but in this volume I have wanted to emphasize the lion aspect, probably because I need more of that in my own life. I find, as I explore the world of Rumi's work, that I keep discovering those qualities with which I need attunement.

Coleman Barks

The Gazelle

A hunter captures a gazelle and puts it
in the stable with the cows and donkeys.

The gazelle runs about wild with fear and confusion.
Every night the man pours out chopped-up straw
for the barn animals. They love it,
but the gazelle shies quickly from side to side
in the big stall, trying to get away
from the smokey dust of the straw
and from the animals milling to eat it.

Whoever has been left for a time
with those who are different
will know how forsaken
this gazelle feels.

Solomon loved the company of the hoopoe.
"Unless she has a valid excuse to be absent,
I will punish her for not being here
with the worst punishment there is."

And what might that be? What this gazelle
is going through: to be confined somewhere
apart from your own kind.

The soul is that way in the body,
a royal falcon put in with crows.
It sits here and endures what it must,
like a great saint, like an Abu Bakr,
in the city of Sabzawar.

Once the great King Muhammed Khwarizm
beseiged Sabzawar. They gave up easily.
"Whatever you require as tribute we will give."

"Bring me a holy person, someone who lives
united with God, or I will harvest
your inhabitants like corn."

They brought sacks of gold. They knew that
no one in Sabzawar lived in that state.
"Do you think I am still a child
that I should be fascinated with coins?"

For three days and nights
they called through the town
looking for an Abu Bakr.

Finally, they saw a traveler
lying in a ruined corner of a wall,
sick and exhausted.

Immediately, they recognized a True Person.
"Get up! The king wants to see you.
You can save our lives!"

"I'm not supposed to be here.
If I could walk, I would already have arrived
in the city where my friends are."

They lifted him above their heads on a board
like corpses are carried on
and bore him to the king.

Sabzawar is this world,
where a True Person wastes away,
apparently worthless,

yet all the king wants from Sabzawar
is such a one. Nothing else will do.

Muhammed says, "God does not look at outward forms,
but at the love within your love."

The *Qalb*, the inner heart, that space
in which seven hundred universes
are just a lost speck,

we're looking for *that* in the small,
seedy town of Sabzawar! And sometimes,
we find it.

One who has that love is a six-sided mirror
through which God can look at *us*, here.

The gifts come through such a one.
His palm opens without conditions.
That union cannot be said.

I leave this subject with you.

Wealthy people bring money.
God says, "Bring devotion to one
whose loving mixes with mine."

That love is what God wants.
That love is a mother and a father
to us and is the origin of every creature.

You might say, "Lord,
I have brought this heart-love."

"Qutu, an ordinary town in Turfan
is full of this kind of love. Instead
bring the Qalb of the Qutb, the soul
of the soul of the soul of Adam."

God waits for that.
One may wander days in Sabzawar
and not see such a being.

The noblest native in Sabzawar might come,
and God would say, "Why do you offer this
rotting corpse? Bring the inner love
of one who can save Sabzawar".

Just the sight of them together,
a native of Sabzawar and a True Human Being,
who might be traveling through,
is painful. Yet sometimes they talk.

A townsperson may behave kindly
toward a *Qalb*-person, but it's almost always
hypocrisy. He nods and says *yes*.
He acts sincere, but he's really tricky,
and looking for an advantage.

If the saint accepts his hypocrisy,
he's saved, and that often happens.
The holy ones love to buy damaged goods,
and turn lying into truth.

If someone's trickery seems charming to you,
remember he is only *your* saint, not a real one.
Someone who is like you will often sound prophetic.

Renounce sensuality, so you can sharpen
your spiritual sense. Your olfactory nerve
has been deadened. You cannot catch the fragrance
of sweet musk or ambergris. It's as though
they no longer exist for you.

All this time, our gazelle
has been running back and forth in the stable!

For many days this precious animal
wriggles like a fish thrown up on dry ground.
Like dung and rare incense closed
side by side in a box.

One donkey says sarcastically, "This guy is wild!
He must be somebody special!"

Another, "With all his ebb and flow, he must be
making a pearl. Probably a cheap one."

Another, "Why can't he eat what we eat?"

Another donkey gets indigestion and offers
the gazelle his fodder with a formal invitation.

"No thank you. I am unwell too."

The donkey is offended. "Don't be so aloof.
Are you afraid of what people will say
if you're seen eating with me?"

The gazelle doesn't answer, but he thinks,
"Your food is for *you*. It revives your strength.
But I have known a pasture by a creek
where hyacinths and anemones and sweet basil grow.
My food is there. Some destiny put me here,
but I can't forget the other. If my body
gets old and sick, still my spirit
can stay new."

The donkey seems to know what the gazelle
is thinking. "Yes, anyone can brag
in a strange country. Who's to know?"

The gazelle, "This musk gland identifies me,
but no one here has a nose tuned to that scent.
Donkeys like to smell donkey urine on the road,
and that's about all."

Muhammed says, "True surrender is odd
in this world. Even 'Islamic' relatives
avoid a perfect saint."

He or she may look human, but there's a lion nature
inside. If you are a cow, and you try to be friends
with such a one, you'll be torn to pieces, instantly.

In fact, you'll become a lion!
If you're happy being a cow, stay away.

Potiphar, the king of Egypt, in a dream once
saw with his spiritual eye seven well-nourished cows
and seven lean cows that came and ate the fat cows.

Lean cows are lions inside,
like a True Person who can detach you completely
from the dregs of your cow-nature

and make you so pure and spacious
that your foot touches Orion's belt.

How long will I keep caw-talking like a crow?

Husam, why did you kill *your* rooster?

"Because I began to hear
the Friend's voice
inside me."

A rooster loves lust, and lust again,
and instant satisfaction of lust,
that poisonous, cheap wine.

If it weren't necessary for procreation, Adam
would have castrated himself in shame
over his own lechery.

Satan comes to God and says,
"I need some powerful bait."

God gives him gold and silver
and herds of beautiful horses.

"Bravo!" says Satan, but his lip drops,
and he screws up his lemon face.

God throws in the other precious metals
and the gemstones.

"Oh thank you! And might there be anything else
around here that I could use?"

God gives the marbled meats,
and the tasty sherbets,
and the silk robes.

"But I need something that will hold and keep holding
like a rope woven of palm-fiber,
so that your holy people can show their holy strengths
by bursting something *very* powerful.
I want an even more cunning lure."

God brings wine and a harp.
Satan smiles a crooked half-smile.
Those are not *exactly* what he had in mind.

Then suddenly, as though a dry path appeared
through the Red Sea, Satan saw the beauty of women,
and he began to dance. "More! More!"

The hazy eyes, the fascination of a soft cheek,
a cheekbone, a reddening lip, the *glance*
that burns a man like a cumin seed
on a hot fire-brick!

A young woman's light, coquettish half-walk half-run
springs to Satan's eyes like a revelation of divine glory,
and a lifting of the veil.

Some comment on the text, *We created man and woman
in the best physical and mental proportion,
and then We reduced them to the lowest of the low.*

The garden beauty, to which the angels bowed down,
after a time, was dragged by the hair
by Gabriel and led *out*.

Why? Why was paradise lost?
Why does a date-palm lose its leaves in autumn?
Why does every beautiful face grow in old age
wrinkled like the back of a Libyan lizard?
Why does a full head of hair get bald?
Why is the tall, straight figure
that divided the ranks like a spear
now bent almost double?

The bright-red anemone grows saffron.
Lion strength weakens to nothing.
The wrestler who could hold anyone down
is led out with two people supporting him,
their shoulders under his arms.

These are all messages from the fall.
What fault was committed?

God answers,
              "The crime is
that they put on borrowed robes
and pretended they were theirs.

I take the beautiful clothes back,
so that you will learn the robe
of appearance is only a loan."

The sheaf-stack belongs to God.
Human beings are gleaners.
Rays from the sun.

The earth-colored glass
makes everything seem diverse,
but that glass eventually shatters.

Your lamp was lit from another lamp.
All God wants is your gratitude for that.

Lend, is the divine command.
Make God a loan from your existence,
and see what fortunes accumulate!

Diminish a little, for your own sake,
all this eating and drinking, and watch
a new basin fill in front of you.

Then God may say, "Death,
give back what you took."

But you'll turn away.
You won't want those things.

Sufis throw away their wantings and their objects.
They abandon pieces of clothing in the dance,
and those articles are never returned.

They are given to the singer,
or divided among the dancers.

They rise from a briny, annihilating
ocean into pure clarity.

They confront the world openly with its arrogance
and its hypocrisy. They are warriors
for non-existence.

The planter works with most joy
whose barn is completely empty,
the planter who works for that
which has not appeared.

Second by second I know you're expecting
some sure understanding, some spiritual perception,
some peace, but I am not allowed to say
more about this mystery,

or else I would create a Baghdad
in the wilds of the Georgia mountains,
and there would be no more doubting!

(*Mathnawi*, V, 833-973,979-995,1002-1025)

Seashell Toys

Go into God's qualities
and God's face.

Empty into those and be there,
and not there, as when letters elide
and disappear into each other
to make a smooth connection.

In the uniting
they are *silent*.

The words, *You did not throw when you threw*,
were spoken without Muhammed's speaking them.

The words, *God said*,
spring from silence.

A medicine on the shelf is medicinal
only when it dissolves into a diseased body.

Even if every tree were cut and split
and every limb and splinter made into pens,
and even if the ocean were ink and every human being
joined in the work, there would still be no hope
for finishing this *Mathnawi*!

But as long as the brickmaker's mould stays filled
with clay, this poetry will keep building.

When there's no more clay, use water!
When there's no more land-forests,
use ocean-forests!

Muhammed said, "Talk about the ocean for a while.
Then turn toward land, pick up a toy,
and talk about toys."

Children love their seashell toys,
and with them they learn about the ocean,
because a little piece of ocean
inside the child, and inside the toy,
knows the whole ocean.

(*Mathnawi*, VI, 2239-2256)

The Lion's Shoulder

The Jesus of your spirit is inside you now.
Ask that one for help, but don't ask for body-things,
like the foolish young man in the story,
who insisted that Jesus put a body back
around some bones that he had found.

Don't ask Moses for provisions
that you can get from Pharoah.

Don't worry so much about livelihood.
Your livelihood will turn out as it should.
Be constantly occupied instead
with listening to God.

Jesus pronounced the Name over the pile of bones,
and a black lion sprang back into being, swung once
with its paw, and tore the young man's skull open.
The brain-kernel was scattered and smashed.

Jesus asked the lion, "Why did you maul him
so quickly?"
                    "Because he was troubling you."
"Why didn't you drink the blood?"

                    Many people
are like this lion. They rage with hunger
and then they leave the world without
having eaten what they killed.

They have the material means,
but they stay unsatisfied.

The lion explained, "Killing this man
was a warning to others. I have been dead.
There is no food now for me in this place."

The lion's swift attack is the right punishment
for those who insult the spirit, for those
who find a pure stream and then urinate in it.

If you know the nature of the stream,
bow your head down inside it.

A person meets a prophet
and somehow doesn't say,
"Lord, help me to *Be*."

How is it that you ask for physical comfort,
and not for a true existence?

Are you dogs that you love bones so?
Are you leeches that you want only blood?

Why are you so blind to what the soul needs?
Weep for yourself as when a cloud weeps,
and then the branch freshens. As when a candle
releases tears and gets brighter.

Wherever people grieve over anything,
you should sit with them and grieve louder,
because you have an even better right to moan.

They lament for what passes away. You cry
for your forgetting what doesn't.

You have been imitating spirituality.

Imitation is a lock on your chest.
Dissolve it with tears.

Imitation may be as small as a piece of straw,
or as huge as a mountain. Imitation
is a blind man describing a landscape
with beautiful words. There's no heart-knowledge.

The blind man gets excited with the words,
but you feel the *distance* between him and the beauty.

The imitator is a riverbed.
He doesn't *drink* the water.

It just passes through him on its way
to the water-drinkers. The riverbed
is not thirsty. Nothing stays there.

The imitator is a flute
that sounds pitiful
in order to be bought.

The imitator is a professional mourner,
with no motive but money. The words burn,
but there's no warmth, and no broken-open-ness.

The difference between being with a true knower
and being with an imitator is like
the difference between being
in the actual presence of the prophet David
and being outside somewhere hearing
a vague echo sound.

David is a source. The imitator
has just memorized some psalms.

Do not be fooled. The ox pulls the load,
while the cart makes a creaking noise.

Though even the imitator gets some reward,
as professional mourners get their wages.

But if the imitation-saint could distinguish
between God as God is, and "God" as he says the word,
he would dissolve all interest in self-interest.

For years he carries the *Qur'an* around,
hoping to make a living by being holy.

Had those words been written inside him,
his body would have shivered into particles.

In sorcery there are demonic helpers
who find ways to make you successful.

You have been doing such things
with the name of God.

A farmer once tied his ox in the stable.
A lion came and ate the ox
and lay down in its place!

The farmer went out late at night
to check on the ox. He felt in the corner
and rubbed his hand along the flank of the lion,
up the back, feeling the shoulder, and around
the chest to the other shoulder.

The lion thinks, "If a light were lit
and this man could suddenly see,
he would die of the discovery.

He's stroking me so familiarly,
because he thinks I'm his ox."

So the imitator doesn't realize
what he's fooling with . God thinks,
"You fake. Sinai crumbled and split
with jets of blood streaming from it
for the sake of the name
that you say so thoughtlessly.

You learned it from your mother and father,
not from your own experience."

If you are *not* an imitator,
your ego will dissolve, and you
will become a voice in the air.

(*Mathnawi,* II, 450-512)

The Grasses

The same wind that uproots trees
makes the grasses shine.

The lordly wind loves the weakness
and the lowness of grasses.
Never brag of being strong.

The axe doesn't worry how thick the branches are.
It cuts them to pieces. But not the leaves.
It leaves the leaves alone.

A flame doesn't consider the size of the woodpile.
A butcher doesn't run from a flock of sheep.

What is form in the presence of reality?
Very feeble. Reality keeps the sky turned over
like a cup above us, revolving. Who turns
the sky-wheel? The universal intelligence.

And the motion of the body comes
from the spirit like a waterwheel
that's held in a stream.

The inhaling-exhaling is from spirit,
now angry, now peaceful.
Wind destroys, and wind protects.

There Is No Reality But God,
says the completely-surrendered sheikh,
who is an ocean for all beings.

The levels of creation are straws in that ocean.
The movement of the straws comes from an agitation
in the water. When the ocean wants the straws calm,
it sends them close to shore. When it wants them
back in the deep surge, it does with them
as the wind does with the grasses.

                              This never ends.

(*Mathnawi*, I, 3325-3343)

The Thicket

Don't burn a blanket because of one flea!
Don't waste a day on trivial irritation,
some gnat's headache.

Take your attention off the forms
and focus on what's inside.

If you're on this way, choose companions
who are also pilgrims. No matter their shape,
color, or national origin, if they are *your* people,
go with them.
                This confused story,
like the doings of lovers, may be told up and down
and sideways, because it's not a story.

It has no beginning or end. It's water.
Each incident-drop is self-contained, and yet not.

This is just the bare cash of how we are
in this instant, you and I.

A sufi sees that whatever happened in the past
is completely gone. In that last story we told,
we are all now the man with his gift of water,
and the generous caliph, and the jug.

Know this: there's a marriage in each of us.
One partner is reason, universal clarity.
The other is desire and ambition. Those qualities
darken the candles of reason.

How did this come to be? It happens
because the whole has parts, and the parts
are not *in relation* to the whole as the smell
of the rose remains somehow *part* of the rose.

And with the rose that I'm talking about,
all the growing things are inside it, just
as the turtledove's coo enters and *becomes*
the nightingale.
                      But if I go more deeply
into this difficult question, will I be able
to give water to those of you who are thirsty?

If you're in some particular trouble,
a tight spot, be patient. Patience
is the way out of anxiety.

And try to avoid distracting thoughts.
Thoughts are like wild donkeys in the thicket
of human existence. Stay away from the market bazaar
of thought-traffic, and find your strength.

Such acts of abstinence are the ultimate medicine.
Let these words enter your open ear,
and they will become a gold earring.

And then you will become a ring around the moon
ascending toward the Pleiades.

Know that created beings are as diverse as Z
and A. From one perspective unified.
From another, they seem opposites.

To one being, resurrection is laughter.
To another, it's a deadly judging-time,
when all frauds will be exposed.

A thorn loves the fall, because then he knows
that he won't be compared to the rose,
but the gardener knows, and a True Human Being
is always saying, "Look, it's spring!"

The body is here blooming and shining,
because form must *be*,
and then be dropped, before the knobs
of spiritual fruit can appear.

Bread must be broken, before it gives us strength.
Clusters of grapes must be crushed
to make wine. Myrobalan
must be pounded into powder,
so it can heal.
                        Husam! Take out two clean
sheets of paper. Add a description
of the true sheikh. Your slender body
is so frail, but without the gift of your spirit-sun
we could see nothing. You are the wick,
the end of the thread, the clue we follow.

Write about the guide,
the summer full-moon.

Husam is young, but the truth has made him so old
that he has no birthdate. Old wine and old gold
are the most precious. Find such a teacher,
because without one you're in danger.
You need an escort on this mountain road.
If you go alone, you'll get dizzy
with the ghoul-sounds.

Read the *Qur'an* where it tells about
these bits of bone and hair
that we find by the roadside.

Keep the reins tight, or your donkey will stray.
And if you do leave the road, go in the opposite direction
from where your donkey wants to go.

That will get you back on the path.
Don't be constant friends
with sexual desire.

Stay with those who have a true guide.
Their company protects.

(*Mathnawi*, I, 2892-2959)

Various Disguises and Scams

A bird lit in a meadow where a trap was set.
Grain had been put out on the ground,
and nearby a fowler had wrapped himself in grass
and pulled roses and red anemones over his head like a cap.

The bird had some notion that this clump of grass
was not all grass, but at first look,
he had no argument about what it might be.

He hopped a circuit around the strange heap
and asked,
                    "Who are you, out here in the wild?"

"I am a renunciate,
content to live like the grass.
After my neighbor's death, I closed my shop.
I gave up associating with every human being
that came along, and now I'm trying to be a friend
of the One. I saw that my jaw
would eventually be bound in the shroud,
so I figured it was best to use it less now.

You birds wear beautiful green robes
with gold embroidery, but at the end
you too will be wrapped in unsewn cloth."

All faces turn back into dirt.
The moist-dry, hot-cold parts
rejoin their kinfolk, and our spirits
receive a letter from the world
of pure intelligence. It says,

> *So your five-day buddies left you!*
> *Learn who your true friends are.*

Some children, when they're playing with strangers,
get so hot and preoccupied with the game,
that they take off their shirts. Night comes,
and their clothes are gone, stolen.

It's impossible to play in the dark,
and now they're afraid to go home.

You've heard the line,
This present life is a play.

You've thrown off your clothes in the fun of living.
They floated away in the wind,
and now you're scared.

While it's still day, I've realized
that men are thieves, and that most of life
is wasted, half in looking for a lover,
and half in worrying over the plots
of our enemies. The former desiring
carries off our cloaks, and the latter
anxiety takes our caps.
                        Yet we remain
completely and obliviously absorbed
in our play. It's getting dark.

Death is near. Leave the game.
Saddle the horse of remorse
and catch up with the thief.

Get your clothes back. That confession-horse
is the speediest there is.

But keep it tied safely
when you're with the thief.

A certain man on his way to the village
has a ram that he leads along behind him.

A thief sneaks up and cuts the halter rope.
Finally the man notices and runs left and right
looking for the lost ram.
                          He sees the thief
beside a well, though he doesn't know
that it's the thief. The ram is elsewhere.
He goes to ask if he's seen a loose ram.

The thief is kneeling by the well crying.
"What's the matter?"
                          "My purse has fallen in.
If you can help me get it out, I'll give you
a fifth of everything in it. You could soon have
one-fifth of a hundred gold dinars
in your hand!"
                          The man thinks, "That's enough
to buy ten rams! One door is shut,
and God opens ten new doors."

He slips out of his clothes and climbs down
into the well, where there is nothing, of course,
and the thief carries away his clothes.

Oh, it takes a prudent man
to make it into the village!

When one loss causes a greedy panic,
then more losses are liable to come.

Imposters appear in many disguises.
Stay in your refuge with God,
and they won't deceive you.

(*Mathnawi*, VI, 435-477)

The Earthquake That Frees Prisoners

Bestami said, "All these years,
people have thought they've been listening to me,
but I haven't said a thing.
            The Speaker speaks.
I am only an echo."

The wall says to the nail,
"Why are you splitting me?"

"It's not me," says the nail.
"Look above me."

Don't beg the spear-shaft for mercy.
Ask the one who holds it.

The One that shapes me
as Azar did images.

He makes a cup. I hold liquid.
A dagger. I cut.
A fountain. Come to me for water.
He lights a fire. I give off heat.
He makes me rain. I come up in cornstalks.
He makes an arrow. I pierce the body.
A snake. I salivate mouth-venom.

A friend. I do kind services.
I am a pen between those fingers,
so I don't tremble, wondering
what to do.

This is how Azrael talked to the earth,
and while he did, as a magician distracts
his audience, he stole a handful of dirt
and brought the handful back to God
as a runaway is brought back to school.

God said, "I'll make you the Angel of Death,
the executioner of my creatures."

"But Lord, they'll think I'm their enemy
when I strangle them."
                              "I'll turn their attention
away from you and toward the diseases
and the woundings and all the many ways
they have to die."
                              "But there are some who see
beyond the secondary causes of fever and dysentery.
They know the divine decree.

All diseases have a cure, as being cold
can be cured by a fur coat. But when
the decree comes, no amount of wrapping in clothes
can keep the fated one from freezing.
There are some who know that."
                              "Azrael,
even if they *see* you, remember, *you*
are a secondary cause too. *I am nearer.*"

Death is not bitter to those who know.
If an earthquake opens the prison walls,
do you think an escaping prisoner
will complain of the damage done
to the stone and marble-work?

No prisoner yet has talked such nonsense.
The soul soars when it's freed from the body,
like a convict in his cell sleeping,
dreaming of a rose garden.

He knows he's dreaming, and he doesn't want
to go back into his body, his dungeon.

He prays, "Let me keep walking here like a prince."
God says, "Yes. Your prayer is granted.
Do not go back." He dies in his sleep
and stays in that rose-paradise,
with no regrets for what he's left
back in the prison cell.

Stand under the pointed arch and weep.
Burn all night like a candle being beheaded
in its own flame. Close your lips
to food and drink. Hurry
to this other table, trembling
like a willow. Forget your weaknesses.
Your longing is everything.

People will say, "So-and-so is dead."
But you'll know how alive you've become.

The spirit is a watercolor world.
This other is a pile of scraps,
a dung-heap of disease. On the material side,
if you eat too little, you get restless.
Too much, and you start farting.
Too little, you get mean and anemic.
Too much, you're grumpy with indigestion.

Spiritual food makes you light and pure.
Be patient. Persist in fasting.
Expect the food of God to arrive.

A full-fed man does not expect anything.
A foodless man is always looking.

Expect the best and most noble dishes,
and the Host will bring them out.

A mountain lifts its elegant head
like a guest that receives the dawn.

A certain simpleton was saying, "This place
would be fine, if it weren't for dying."

Answer, "If there were no death, this world
would be just a tangle of straw, a grain-stack
left unthreshed in the field.

What you suppose to be life
is a kind of death, a seed
dropped on unfertile ground.
Nothing comes of it."

Show us everything as it really is.
No one who has died is grieving
because of death. The only grief
is at not being well enough
prepared for dying.

No one objects to exchanging
sour buttermilk for choice wine.

The illuminated life can happen now,
in the moments left. Die to your ego,
and become a True Human Being.

(*Mathnawi,* V, 1683-1771)

Who Is the Teacher?

Describing Bestami's faith
is like trying to thin
varnish with water.

Any comparison is a single dust speck
floating in the light.

And, if I say the unseen sun
is such a fleck,
I have hidden purposes.

You have found some foam,
not the ocean.

If the luminosity of the sheikh's faith
were to actually rise in the East,
everything below the crust of the earth
would become handfuls of mystery, and
everything above, a green lightedness.

Resplendent spirit,
or a body made from the ground,
which is he?

Tell me, uncle! I'm puzzled.
All this light, yet a body!
Who *is* the teacher?

(*Mathnawi*, V, 3400-3408)

One Silver Coin a Day For Forty Days

A sufi entered the battle,
but when his side fell back,
he did not retreat. He stayed
in danger and got wounded.

He bandaged the wound,
and returned to the fight.

He wanted to receive twenty wounds.
He did not want to die easily,
all at once, with one gesture.

A certain man had forty silver coins.
He would take one a day and toss it
into the ditchwater. He was trying
to teach his animal-soul how to give up
greed.
            "Give it up all at once,"
begged the soul, "so I can go into despair
and be delivered from this torture."
                                    "No,"
said the man. *"Deliberation is my way."*

Wounded again and again, the sufi
finally falls and dies into the source
of truth. Many raw, unready men die,
and their animal-souls escape
to the afterlife, but these raw souls
are still thieves. The sword is shattered,
and the horse killed, but the brigand
still lives. Not everyone killed
in battle is a martyred saint.

Die inside your life,
and go on living.

Kill the animal-part with your sword.
The body is your sword.

Let God handle that sword,
and your identity will become
bewilderingly different.

You will still be an eager warrior
with a deft blade, but changed.

When that part dies, empties,
completely empties, God takes its place.

Then your only food
is divine love.

(*Mathnawi*, V, 3810-3830)

The Berry of Relishing

In the time of Shu'ayb a certain man said,
"God has seen everything I've done wrong,
and yet in his kindness, He
hasn't punished me."

God spoke in the mysterious way to Shu'ayb,
"Answer him, 'You say, "God has not
punished me," but the opposite is true.

God has punished, but you are not aware of it.
You are wandering in a wilderness without
direction. You are bound hand and foot.
You're a pot accumulating layers of rust.

You're getting blinder and blinder
to spiritual things. When smoke hits
a new copper pot, one sees the effect
immediately, but with a surface
so blackened as yours, who can tell
when it gets more blackened?

When you quit meditating, the layers of rust
eat into your soul-mirror. There's no sheen.

If you write once on a sheet of paper,
it can be read, but when you scribble
over and over, the script
becomes unreadable.

Dip yourself in the acid that cleans copper.
Lay out your blackenedness clearly.'"

Shu'ayb said this, and with one inbreath,
roses began to bloom in the man's chest.

But he said, "Still, I want a sign
that God has punished me."

God, through Shu'ayb, said, "I will not reveal
your secrets, but I will give you
an indication that you will understand:

You have many devotions to your credit,
much fasting and ritual prayer,
but you haven't *relished* those acts.

There are lots of walnut shells,
but none with a sweet nut inside.

There must be a tastiness,
a seed of delight, or the berry
will not make a sapling that later
becomes a fruit-producing tree.

Joyless practicing without savor
is just fantasy-doing."

(*Mathnawi*, II, 3364-3397)

Let That Laughter Lead You

When you go to buy a pomegranate,
pick the one that's laughing,
that has its rind cleft,
so that through its broken-open-ness
you get some information
about the seeds.

Listen for the laughter
that shows the inside,
that cracks the casket-shell
and lets you see the pearl.

There's another kind, an unhappy laughing
like the red anemone's that shows
its inner blackness.

But pomegranate-laughter is blessed,
like the companionship of good people.

Even if you're a common rock,
when you join them,
you'll become a precious stone.

Keep the love of holy laughing in you.
Don't visit sad neighborhoods. Let
laughter lead you to the right people.

Your body-wantings will take you out of the sunlight
into dark and dank places. Feed on the conversation
of a lover. Look for spiritual growth from one
who is farther along than you.

There was once a Christian gospel
that had in it some mention of Muhammed,
his courage and his fasting.

Whenever a group of Christians studied
this gospel, they bowed and kissed the words
of that passage. Without knowing it,
they were looking for refuge
inside that light, and with its power
it befriended and helped them.

(*Mathnawi*, I, 718-733)

The Flap of the Wallet

The spiritual guide, Omar,
saw that the ambassador from Rum
was able to hear what he said, so he sowed
seed in that well-worked soil.

The ambassador asked, "How is it that
the spirit came *here*? Why did the infinite
bird agree to enter this cage?"

"When God sings and recites over parts
of non-existence that have no ears and no eyes,
that second they dance into existence.

When God sings over beings in existence,
they run quickly back where they came from.

God talks to a rose. It blooms.
To a rock. It changes to transparent crystal.

God speaks kindly to the sun. It shines.
Says a terrible truth. It goes into eclipse.

Consider what must get whispered
in a cloud's ear to make it rain,
or in the ground to make it so quiet.

Whoever looks puzzled, God has told him or her
a new riddle. Caught between possibilities,
take the cotton out of *both* ears.

Your spirit-ear is where inspiration comes in,
the talk that is not heard by your sense ears,
or in rational discourse, or in opinions,
or in compulsions."

Union with God is not
a compulsion. When that wedding happens,
it's like a drop of water entering an oyster,
like blood going into a deer's musk gland.

Don't say such changes cannot happen.
A vast freedom could live inside you.

A loaf of bread wrapped in a cloth for the table
is just an object, but inside a human body
it becomes a gladness for being alive!
The animal-soul transmutes it. Think
what must be the transformative power
of the true soul, and the Soul
within that soul.

A simple piece of humanity takes in intelligence
and cuts through a mountain to find jewels,
or builds a ship to cross the oceans.

That rock-and-mountain-splitting strength
is a likeness for the strength of the soul.

If the love in your chest
could open the flap of the wallet
of this mystery, it would escape quickly
into the distance, and be just a speck.

(*Mathnawi*, I, 1445-1479)

Ascending and Descending

Muhammed said, "Make no distinction
between my ascending and Jonah's descending
into the fish. Nearness to God
is beyond ranking and description."

No *up, down, soon, far,* or *late.*
Those terms are appropriate only
for existence, and time.

In non-existence, being destroyed
is the greatest honor. The best provision
is an emptiness. Poverty, a glorious wealth.

Anyone who feels proud of winning,
or privately glad at the public embarrassment
of someone, he or she is still
caught in the illusion.

(*Mathnawi,* III, 4512-4524)

The Prophet's Vision

Muhammed said, "The bowl fell from the roof,
and I understood this bodily-existence.

I gaze at an unripe grape
and taste the wine.

I look in your inmost self
and see the universe not yet created.

I see your prosperity and your falling.
I see you eating the poison
that will kill you.

I came to waken everyone to action!
You hurry like moths toward the fire, while
I'm waving wildly to keep you from it.

Things you think are triumphs are
the beginnings of unconsciousness.

You've been calling happily to each other
to attack me. You want to throw me over,
but in doing that, you'll fall and be held
down in time, that powerful lion."

(*Mathnawi*, III, 4540-4560)

Neglecting Meditation
and Refusing Kindnesses

When you neglect your meditation,
you contract with pain.

This is God's way of telling you
that your inner pain can become visible.
Don't ignore it.

Your spiritual wincing affects your love.
A thief carrying off someone's property
feels a twinge of conscience.

"What's this?" he asks. Tell him,
"It's the hurt of the one you've hurt,
hurting you." A conscience-seizure
changes easily to a seizure by the police.

Thoughts display themselves.
A pang for being forgetful
is a root. Roots produce branches.

Your inner opening and closing
is the underworld, the ground
that feeds the manifest world.

Tear out the thorn-roots quickly.
When you feel held in, find out why.
Dig for the cause.

When you feel expanded, water that.
When fruits appear, give them to friends.

In Saba, everyone was occupied with foolishness
and dalliance, and it was their habit
to be intentionally ungrateful
to anyone who gave them something.

To any benefactor, a citizen of Saba would say,
"I am annoyed by your kindness.
Go somewhere else with your generosity.
I don't want your gifts."

They prayed, "Lord, be far away.
Our mess is better than your beauty.
Take away the orchards, the lovely women,
your peace and your safekeeping.

The friendly towns closeby, we don't want
such things! We like the desert
with its desolation and its dangers."

Mankind says the same, "We want winter
in the summer, and then winter comes,
and we don't like it. We're poor,
and we want wealth, and we get it,
and it's not enough!

We're given guidance,
and we ignore it."

Man's animal-soul is a pyramidal
thorn-cluster. No matter how it's arranged,
it pierces what it touches.

Burn those thorns.
Stay close to the Friend.

The people of Saba finally carried ingratitude
to its limit. "We love pestilence,"
they cried. "We love our spreading disease
better than any cooling wind."

They began to kill their teachers.
They grew completely deaf to God's will.

The brains of animals know their enemies
by their smell. In the floating dust,
sheep can sense that a wolf
has been near, so they graze elsewhere.
But the people of Saba had lost the ability
to be warned. They had broken their connection
to wisdom, and they got torn to bits.

The shepherd called, but the sheep said,
"Go away. What do we need a shepherd for?
Each of us is shepherd enough for himself.
Everybody's a chief in this tribe!"

The blackbird croaked over their houses.
They never heard. They bound up Gabriel
and ripped his feathers out. A dinner
was set for them, but they handed each other
handfuls of straw from the barn floor.

"Here. Eat this.
This is fancy food."

There is no food
but meeting face to face
with the Friend.

(*Mathnawi*, III, 349-401)

Dervish at the Door

A dervish knocked at a house
to ask for a piece of dry bread,
or moist, it didn't matter.

"This is not a bakery," said the owner.

"Might you have a bit of gristle then?"

"Does this look like a butchershop?"

"A little flour?"

"Do you hear a grinding-stone?"

"Some water?"

"This is not a well."

Whatever the dervish asked for,
the man made some tired joke,
and refused to give him anything.

Finally the dervish ran in the house,
lifted his robe, and squatted
as though to take a shit.

"Hey, hey!"

"Quiet, you sad man. A deserted place
is a fine spot to relieve one's self,
and since there's no living thing here,
or means of living, it needs fertilizing."

The dervish began his own list
of questions and answers.

"What kind of bird are you? Not a falcon,
trained for the royal hand. Not a peacock,
painted with everyone's eyes. Not a parrot,
that talks for sugar cubes. Not a nightingale,
that sings like someone in love.

Not a hoopoe bringing messages to Solomon,
or a stork that builds on a cliffside.

What exactly do you do?
You are no known species.

You haggle and make jokes
to keep what you own for yourself.

You have forgotten the One
who doesn't care about ownership,
who doesn't try to turn a profit
from every human exchange."

(*Mathnawi*, VI, 1250-1267)

The Circle Around the Zero

A lover doesn't figure the odds.

He figures he came clean from God
as a gift without a reason,
so he gives without cause
or calculation or limit.

A conventionally religious person
behaves a certain way
to achieve salvation.

A lover gambles everything, the self,
the circle around the zero! He or she
cuts and throws it all away.

This is beyond
any religion.

Lovers do not require from God any proof,
or any text, nor do they knock on a door
to make sure this is the right street.

They run,
and they run.

(*Mathnawi*, VI, 1967-1974)

Eat! Bread-bird

Being hungry is better
than the maladies that come
with satiety.

Subtlety and lightness
and being true to your devotion
are some of the advantages
of fasting.

A certain person is eating, and greatly
enjoying, a piece of mouldy bread.

Someone asks, "Do you really *like* that food?"

He replies, "When you fast for two days,
a piece of bread tastes like layered pastry.
If I deny my appetite just a little,
I can have halvah every meal."

But fasting is not for everyone,
only those few who become God's lions.

True hunger
is not easy to have,
when fodder is always being set
in front of you with the invitation,

*Eat. You're not a waterbird
that eats air.*

You're a bread-bird. Eat!

(*Mathnawi*, V, 2830-2840)

Sending to the Christian Quarter for Wine - I

When the snow of sensual pleasure
looks at the sun, God's love,
its iciness changes.

It lifts and moves with the breeze.
As David the metalworker makes perfect coats
of chain mail on the water surface,
so snow melts into medicine for the trees.

Except for a pocket here and there
that remains hidden in shade,
locked in itself, saying,
Don't touch me!

Such leftover snow is no friend to anyone,
or to itself, and no help to the greenery.

There was once a great-hearted ruler
who loved wine, and drunkards.

He was a cave of refuge for everyone.
Compassionate, a strong leader,
a knower of secrets, an ocean, and one
who recognized the Friend, immediately.

This was in early Christian times,
when wine was still a sacrament.

One night, an old friend visited this man.
They had no wine, so they sent a servant
to a nearby Christian monk,
who made the choicest wine.

"Take this jar and fill it
with that which releases the soul.

One cup and there is no judging
good and bad, no high or low."

In that Christian wine
there is a secret substance,
just as sovereignty hides
inside a dervish robe,
the black pigment-cloth
covering the gold.

Treasures are not to be openly displayed.
They must be buried like the spirit
of Adam inside earthiness.

The slave ran with his jar to the monastery
and brought the precious Christian wine,
within which emperor and slave
mix equally, where throne and workbench
become each other, like barley
and wheat in a perfect soup.

This was the kind of wine that the servant
was carrying back to the two friends.

Suddenly, an old man, a dry, long-suffering
ascetic, confronted him. "What's in the jar?"

"Wine for my master and his friend."

"Is this the true way? To drink
and become semi-intelligent?

Your intelligence, as it is, is weak.
Consider how it will be when you're drunk.

Do you really think you have enough understanding
to drink wine?   Wine is not for those
who seek the Friend.   That path leads
through a terrible wilderness.
Don't blindfold your guide!

Don't put a thief in the pulpit.
Keep him bound up.   Let your enemy
eat dirt.   Don't bring him wine."

With his long speech over, the ascetic
threw a stone at the jar and broke it.

The servant ran home with nothing.
"Where is the wine?"

He told the whole story,
and the good-hearted man became furious.

"Where is this ascetic
who thinks he can tell everyone
what to do?   The cure for him
is to be beaten on the head
with bull-balls!"

He ran out looking for the character.
But the ascetic heard him coming and hid
beneath a pile of ropemaker's wool.

From under there one could hear muttering,
"Only a perfect steel mirror
can reflect a man's face and tell
its faults, not someone scared
and unhappy, like me."

I am reminded of the court jester from Termid,
a fellow named Dalqak. He was playing chess
with the king one day.

"Checkmate," said Dalqak.

The king picked up each piece and threw it at him.
"Here's *checkmate* for you, you cheat!"

Dalqak feared for his life,
but the king commanded him
to keep playing. Again, the moment.

"Checkmate," said Dalqak,
and ran to the far corner,
and covered himself with six rugs.

"What's going on?" asked the king.

"Checkmate, checkmate, checkmate,"
said Dalqak.

It *is* a problem, how to tell the truth
to someone in an agitated state.

So the man whose wine was spilled
was angrily kicking the old ascetic's door.
Neighbors came out to calm him.

"Don't punish the old guy.
His brain has dried up
with all the self-mortification.

He's tried to meet the Beloved,
but he never has.

That's why he acts as he does. That's why
his eyes are so painful to look into.

He keeps complaining to God, 'All the others
can fly. Why have you cut my wings?'

Where he lives is a narrow stall
that a camel might lie down in at night.

He cannot get up,
or take a deep breath
in there, in his life.

Never hand such a person a knife.
He'll eventually turn his hatred
on himself and rip open his stomach."

(*Mathnawi*, V, 3431-3436,3439-3534)

A Spider Playing in the House

Eyesight becomes vision
after a meeting with the Friend.

Another seeing rises behind the eyes
and looks out *through* the eyes.

This does not happen to a fool.
A fool looks at deadly poison
and sees candy for an idle moment.

What he claims is the obvious road to take
is really the mockery-scream of a ghoul
devouring his ancestors!

A simple, open sky is sometimes
an unsterile lancet
that will give you an infection.

Dear sky, learn mercy.
Change your revolving.

You fed us when we were young,
with the beauty of weather,
and with your fire-baskets,
the star-lanterns, that never
seem to need oil.

Materialists think that you have always existed,
sweet sky, but mystics know your beginnings,
and the prophets have taken us beyond sky-worship.

A spider that plays in a house
does not understand how, or even if,
the house was built, but a man does,
even if he does not know exactly *when*,
or *precisely* the name of the builder.

He doesn't need to spin
a lot of theological cobwebs.

A gnat has no idea who dug and planted
the garden, a gnat born in late spring,
who dies in early fall, or sooner.

A grubworm living in a rotten board
knows nothing of the tree when it was a sapling,
or if the worm does know something,
it would come from the essential intellect
in all existence and not from the worm-form.

There are many guises for intelligence.
One part of you is gliding in a high windstream,
while your more ordinary notions
take little steps and peck at the ground.

Conventional knowledge is death
to our souls, and it is not really *ours*.

It's laid on. Yet we keep saying
that we find "rest" in these "beliefs."

We must become ignorant
of what we've been taught,
and be, instead, bewildered.

Run from what's profitable and comfortable.
If you drink those liqueurs, you'll spill
the springwater of your real life.

Distrust anyone who praises you.
Give your investment money,
and the interest on the capital,
to those who are actually destitute.

Forget safety.
Live where you fear to live.
Destroy your reputation.
Be notorious.

I have tried prudent planning
long enough. From now
on, I'll be mad.

(*Mathnawi*, II, 2309-2332)

Desire and the Importance of Failing

A window opens.
A curtain pulls back.

The lamps of lovers connect,
not at their ceramic bases,
but in their lightedness.

No lover wants union with the Beloved
without the Beloved also wanting the lover.

Love makes the lover weak,
while the Beloved gets strong.

Lightning from here strikes *there*.
When you begin to love God, God
is loving *you*. A clapping sound
does not come from one hand.

A thirsty man calls out, "Delicious water,
where are you?" while the water moans,
"Where is the water-drinker?"

The thirst in our souls *is* the attraction
put out by the Water itself.

We belong to It,
and It to us.

God's wisdom made us lovers of one another.
In fact, all the particles of the world
are in love and looking for lovers.

Pieces of straw tremble
in the presence of amber.

We tremble like iron filings
welcoming the magnet.

Whatever that Presence gives us
we take in. Earth signs feed.
Water signs wash and freshen.
Air signs clear the atmosphere.
Fire signs jiggle the skillet,
so we cook without getting burnt.

And the Holy Spirit helps with everything,
like a young man trying to support a family.
We, like the man's young wife, stay home,
taking care of the house, nursing the children.

Spirit and matter work together like this,
in a division of labor.

Sweethearts kiss and taste the delight
before they slip into bed and mate.

The desire of each lover is
that the work of the other be perfected.
By this man-and-woman cooperation,
the world gets preserved.
Generation occurs.

Roses and blue arghawan flowers flower.
Night and day meet in a mutual hug.

So different, but they do love each other,
the day and the night, like family.

And without their mutual alternation
we would have no energy.

Every part of the cosmos draws toward its mate.
The ground keeps talking to the body,
saying, "Come back! It's better for you
down here where you came from."

The streamwater calls to the moisture in the body.
The fiery aether whispers to the body's heat,
"I am your origin. Come with me."

Seventy-two diseases are caused
by the various elements pulling inside the body.
Disease comes, and the organs
fall out of harmony.

We're like the four different birds,
that each had one leg tied in
with the other birds.

A flopping bouquet of birds!
Death releases the binding, and they fly off,
but before that, their pulling is our pain.

Consider how the soul must be,
in the midst of these tensions,
feeling its own exalted pull.

My longing is more profound.
These birds want the sweet green herbs
and the water running by.

I want the infinite! I want wisdom.
These birds want orchards and meadows
and vines with fruit on them.

I want a vast expansion.
They want profit and the security
of having enough food.

Remember what the soul wants,
because in that, eternity
is *wanting* our souls!

Which is the meaning of the text,
They love That, and That loves them.

If I keep on explaining this,
the *Mathnawi* will run to eighty volumes!

The gist is: whatever anyone seeks,
that is seeking the seeker.

No matter if it's animal,
or vegetable, or mineral.

Every bit of the universe
is filled with wanting,
and whatever any bit wants,
wants the wanter!

This subject must dissolve again.

Back to Sadri Jahan and the uneducated peasant
who loved him, so that gradually Sadri Jahan
loved the lowly man. But who really
attracted who, whoom, Huuuu?

Don't be presumptuous and say one or the other.
Close your lips. The mystery of loving
is God's sweetest secret.

Keep it. Bury it. Leave it here
where I leave it, drawn as I am
by the pull of the Puller
to something else.

You know how it is. Sometimes
we plan a trip to one place,
but something takes us to another.

When a horse is being broken, the trainer
pulls it in many different directions,
so the horse will come to know
what it is to be ridden.

The most beautiful and alert horse is one
completely attuned to the rider.

God fixes a passionate desire in you,
and then disappoints you.
God does that a hundred times!

God breaks the wings of one intention
and then gives you another,
cuts the rope of contriving,
so you'll remember your dependence.

But sometimes, your plans work out!
You feel fulfilled and in control.

That's because, if you were always failing,
you might give up. But remember,
it is by *failures* that lovers
stay aware of how they're loved.

Failure is the key
to the kingdom within.

Your prayer should be, "Break the legs
of what I want to happen. Humiliate
my desire. Eat me like candy.
It's spring, and finally
I have no will."

(*Mathnawi*, III, 4391-4472)

You Are the Only Student You Have

You are the only faithful student you have.
All the others leave eventually.

Have you been making yourself shallow
with making others eminent?

Just remember, when you're in union,
you don't have to fear
that you'll be drained.

The command comes to *speak*,
and you feel the ocean
moving through you.
Then comes, *Be silent*,
as when the rain stops,
and the trees in the orchard
begin to draw moisture
up into themselves.

(*Mathnawi*, V, 3195-3219)

Sending to the Christian Quarter
for Wine - II

In the middle of a banquet
the prince sent his servant
to the Christian quarter,
where the best wine was sold.

Christians always make
the most delicious wine!

But on the way back the servant
met a Christian ascetic,
who broke the jug with a stone.

"Who does he think he is,
that he should keep me from drinking wine?"
said the prince when he heard.

"Lions walk past me cautiously,
but this tightmouthed fart presumes
to interrupt my guests and me at table.

He spills a liquid more precious
than his own blood, and now
he hides like a woman.

Let him run. The arrow of revenge
will tear between his wings
and pin him to the rocks.

Hypocrites like him are pimps
to their own fears.
They must be struck down!"

His rage, building like a fire
from his mouth, blinded him.

Several of the old Christian's neighbors came
and kissed the prince's hands and bowed
to touch his feet. They were trying to save
the old man from certain, and immediate, death.

One of those kind people said, "Don't shoot
the vengeance-arrow, my prince!

The wine is gone, but you yourself
are delicious enough without that!

Wine derives its taste
from *your* goodness.

Be a king, and remember your father,
and his father, and his.

Drunkenness aspires to be as you already are.
The rosiness of your face at dawn
is the perfect rosé.

You are the whole ocean.
Why send out for a sip of dew?

It's like the sun asking for help with shining
from a dust-mote that only sparkles
a moment in an open window.

Read the inscription on your crown:

  We Honor the Sons of Adam

And what's engraved across your chest,

  We Have Given You....

A True Human Being is the essence,
the original cause.

The world and the universe
are secondary effects.

Don't trade yourself for something worth less!
Existence is in service to you.

And yet you look in books for knowledge.
Ridiculous.

You buy halvah to have some sweetness.
Absolutely absurd!

Everything you want and need
is inside you.

What is wine?
What is music?
What is sex?

When you look to those for delight,
it is as though Venus, the source
of poetry and song and all feasting,
came and begged to have a cup
of the raw, bitter wine that
people drink on the streets.

You are the unconditioned spirit
trapped in conditions,
the sun in eclipse.

It's a shame,
and a great waste."

The neighbor finished his wise appeal,
but the prince was stubborn.

"I don't want your inner wine.
I want the one that makes me reel
like a willow back and forth,

numb to fearing and hoping, swaying
with just whatever breeze."

Good prince, don't be satisfied with *that*.
Getting drunk is a stupid entertainment, or worse.

Think how it is whispering in bed with your lover.
Now think that you're lying there
with a faceless corpse.

The difference in those two scenes
is how self-insulting and *unnatural*
it is, what you want from wine.

(*Mathnawi*, V, 3553-3590)

Doing Donkey Work

There are those of you
who love intellectual things
and consider yourselves superior
to lovers of more solid forms.

Remember how your brightness is borrowed
from the universal intelligence.

Your mental brilliance,
like your physical beauty,
is a thin outer layer.

They're not your reality.
Remember how a beautiful sweetheart
grows old and withers.

Little by little, intellect and physique
decline. There is another beauty,
a love-center with lips that taste
the living water. In *that* drinking
the water and the giver of water
and the drunken one are one.

This has nothing to do with clever figuring.
It has to do with service to God.
Quit talking about it!

You're like a poet who listens
for the arrangement of rhymes,
and not to what's being said.

Reality is a rapture
that takes you out of form,
not a feeling that makes you
more fascinated with forms.

There are those who embroider the saddle
and pay little attention to their donkey.

Keep your donkey under control,
and the pack-saddle will be there.

Tend to your vital heart,
and all you worry about will be solved.

Your donkey is afraid of work.
Tie it up, and make it carry many loads
of patience and gratitude for a hundred years,
or thirty, or twenty.

Don't think to have a harvest unless you plant!
That's the raw hoping of adolescence.
It will make you sick.

Don't say to yourself, "But So-and-so *found*
a treasure and doesn't have to work!"

That may be true, but it rarely
happens, and out of blind luck.

A treasure follows behind your doing daily work.
Don't postpone that with "ifs"!

"If this had happened," or "If I could have...."
Hypocrites die saying those sentences,
and such a death is the deepest grief there is.

(*Mathnawi*, II, 710-738)

Fake Friends

God's heart is a hawk
living in a city of crows,
with a deep loneliness
for companions.

When one of the crows seems friendly,
it's hypocrisy, as when someone says "yes"
after a long warning. He doesn't mean it.
He just wants the admonishing to stop.

He stands with those who have genuinely changed,
but that's the way it is in this market.
Damaged goods get thrown in with the others.

Fly to the love-hawk,
and be its friend.

Any other
is a fake.

There's a subtle fragrance that will come to you
when you're in that one's presence.

You dull that sense
when you live with crows.

(*Mathnawi*, V, 896-906)

Tending Two Shops

Don't run around this world
looking for a hole to hide in.

There are wild beasts in *every* cave!
If you live with mice,
the cat-claws will find you.

The only real rest comes
when you're alone with God.

Live in the nowhere that you came from,
even though you have an address here.

That's why you see things in two ways.
Sometimes you look at a person
and see a cynical snake.

Someone else sees a joyful lover,
and you're both right!

Everyone is half and half,
like the black and white ox.

Joseph looked ugly to his brothers,
and most handsome to his father.

You have eyes that see from that nowhere,
and eyes that judge distances,
how high and how low.

You own two shops,
and you run back and forth.

Try to close the one that's a fearful trap,
getting always smaller. Checkmate,
this way. Checkmate, that.

Keep open the shop
where you're not selling fish-hooks anymore.
You *are* the free-swimming fish.

(*Mathnawi*, II, 590-593,602-613)

At Dawn

One of the traditions of the Prophet
says that on Resurrection Day,
Everybody will be called to rise.

"Children of Adam, lift your heads
up out of the grave!"

Each soul will rejoin its body,
as your consciousness returns to you
at dawn. Daybreak:

the spirit recognizes where it lives
and slips back into the ruin like a jewel
hiding itself in the desert.

The goldsmith's soul knows the goldsmith's body,
and goes there, not to the tailor.

The scholar's soul, back to the scholar.
The dictator's soul, back to him.

Divine knowing makes each spirit
recognize the appropriate body,
as a lamb finds its mother at dawn,
among the others, as your foot
finds its shoe in the dark.

Dawn is a practice-resurrection.
Be with God then,

and you'll know what the *real*
resurrection will be like.

(*Mathnawi*, V, 1772-1780)

Joseph in Prison

Joseph in prison asked a fellow prisoner,
"When you leave here, your affairs will prosper
with the king. Please mention me to him
and try to obtain my release."

One prisoner cannot free another prisoner,
and except for rare cases, every human being
is a prisoner, waiting.

Joseph asked a low, prickly shrub,
like camels graze on, for help,
and he was punished for it.

The prisoner forgot Joseph's name completely,
and Joseph spent several more years confined.

In bright sunlight, don't ask a bat for directions.
If you're an ocean storm, don't look to heat-mirages
and sand for assistance. Don't make a brace
from rotten wood.

God punished Joseph, or seemed to.
Actually He totally absorbed him
in such an intimate joy that
the dungeon disappeared.

There's no more restricted place
than the bloodwalls of the womb,
yet in there God opens a window
into the Presence, and your senses grow.

They blossom out of the body.
The delight is so profound in the womb
that you never want to leave.

You pull toward your mother's spine,
and away from the labia-door.

The way of spiritual pleasure is *inward*.
Don't look for it outside in property or wealth.
Setting means nothing. One man sits ecstatically
in a bare stone nook. Another is sad
in a beautiful rose garden.

At the wine-feast the drunkard
is most happy when he passes out.

Look at his smile. Be a ruin.
This body-house is full of imagery.
Demolish it. Those fantasy art-works
keep you from union.

But the beauty of the pictures
comes from the radiance of the soul!

That light-filled water *produces*
the bubbles that obscure its surface.

That which blocks us from seeing
is from a deep vision-source inside.

Let your bats fly into that sun
and lose their batness!

(*Mathnawi*,VI,3400-3431)

The Two-Way Pull of Freewill and the Freedom of the Involuntary Ball

God's radiance, Husam, polisher of the soul,
Husamuddin, give this *Mathnawi* a free and open course.
Let its fables be as alive as actual living is,
so that the words can become soul
and go inside and work.

Through you, these stories come from the unseen.
They walk into this word-trap and agree
to be confined. Let your life be like Khidr's,
always helping others to grow.

Like Khidr and Elijah,
you stay in the world doing the work
of transforming matter into spirit.

I can't even say a hundredth of what you do.
I can only hint at describing the state
of those who benefit.

Many fall in love with the Creator,
but many also hesitate to choose union.

Bu Talib, Muhammed's uncle, was one of these.
He said, "My nephew is changing the traditional
practices. What will people think of me?"

Uncle, just whisper one profession of faith,
so I can take it to God for you.

"But you know how secrets get around.
Whatever two people share quickly becomes
common knowledge. I'll look like a fool."

How can this faint-hearted hesitation
exist simultaneously with God's
drawing you toward freedom?

Freewill is the perplexity of being pulled
in opposite directions, an ambush on the way.
O Destination of both pullers, help us!

This two-way way,
duality, feels
like a fight.

This oneness path
feels like a banquet.

God explains in the *Qur'an*, *They shrank
from bearing it*, meaning that,
when God offered the trust of freewill
to the rest of the universe, they refused,
fearing it, but humanity accepted.

Now we are constantly questioning,
"Is this better, or that?
Will I fail, or succeed?"

The tide ebbs and flows,
else the ocean would be still.

Source that gave this perplexity,
unperplex me! I'm a skinny camel
with unbalanced baskets on my back.
The panniers slip from side to side.

Freewill scrapes a bad sore on me!
Let the baskets drop off.

When that happens, I'll look up,
and there will be the meadow of union,
where I won't have to decide
which of ten roads to take.

I can just roll around anywhere,
involuntarily, like a ball.

(*Mathnawi*, VI, 183-218)

A New Life

Be like Ibrahim, the king who abdicated
and went to the other kingdom.

At night, when he slept, guards
were patroling the roof, protecting him,
they thought. But his real security
was the justice of his decisions.

And he loved to listen to music, the voices
singing, the strings of the rebeck,
the low menace of the drum, the clear
flute, the trumpet.

Wise men and women have said that we love music
because it *resembles* the sphere-sounds of union.

We've been part of that harmony before,
so these moments of treble and bass
keep our remembering fresh.

But how can this happen within these dense bodies
full of doubt and forgetfulness and grieving?

It's like water passing through the body,
how it becomes stale and bitter,
yet still retains watery qualities.

It will still put out a fire!
And there is a music flowing
through us that can douse
the burning restlessness.

Listening to these melodies,
we strengthen that.

So Ibrahim was resting at night,
and he heard footsteps on the roof.

"Who could this be? Spirits?"

A marvelous group of beings
put their heads down over the roof-edge,
"We're looking for camels!"

"Whoever heard of camels on a roof?"

"Yes. And whoever heard of trying
to be in union with God while
acting as a head of state?"

That's all it took for Ibrahim.
He was gone, vanished.

His beard and his robe were there,
but his real self was on an ecstatic
dervish retreat on Mt. Qaf.

Everyone still brags of what he did.
This world is proud of those
who suddenly change.

There are these people who remember,
who return in sleep to Hindustan.

If you're not one of those elephants,
let the spiritual alchemists,
who are all around us, change you
into one. Every night they touch us
in different ways. New plants
spring up in our awarenesses!

Ibrahim was one of these who dreamed
of the true reality and freed himself.

Muhammed said that the sign of this happening
is that one loses interest in illusory happiness.

This was how it was once for a young prince.
Age has no bearing on this transformation.

He saw, suddenly, that the world was a big game
of king of the mountain: boys scrambling
on a pile of sand. One gets to the top
and calls out, "I am the king!"
Then another throws him off
and makes his momentary claim,
and then another, and so on.

These world-complications can become
very simple, very quickly.

No words are necessary
to see into reality.

Just *be*,
and It is.

(*Mathnawi*, IV, 717-744,829-838,3070-3085)

Arrangements to Meet

Friends, the Beloved is a lion.
We are a deer that has a bad leg
and can't run. Cornered, with no way
to escape, in those arms, the most
we can do is give up.

The Beloved is like the sun,
that neither eats nor sleeps,
saying, *Come, be one with me.*
You have known me before.
You've been expecting me.

One cat waits and watches a mouse-hole,
because that's where it's been fed before.

Another prowls the roof,
because it once caught a bird up there.

One man's attention points toward
the weaver's craft. Another's toward
the palace guard. Still another
has no work. He turns toward
the non-space, the no-time world,
because the Friend once fed him there.

His work is the work of loving God.
All the rest is children playing till dark comes,
and then they disperse. They each go home to sleep.

God says to the soul, "I am the noise of water,
rain coming. You are so thirsty.
How can you fall asleep?"

There was a lover who had been very faithful
to his love for years. One day that friend
said, "Tonight, I have cooked string beans
for you. Meditate in your room until midnight.
Then, I will come and bring you a supper."

The lover offered sacrifices
and distributed loaves of bread,
recognizing how he'd been blessed.
That night he sat as he had been told to,
and at midnight the friend came,
but found the lover asleep!

The friend tore off a little piece
of the lover's sleeve and put
some walnuts in his lap saying,

You are a child.
Play with these!

At dawn the lover woke suddenly,
saw the torn sleeve and the walnuts,
and thought, "Whatever comes to us
comes from our own forgetfulness."

The Beloved we want is always awake,
and always meets us when we arrange to meet.

True lovers get their walnuts ground in the mill!
They don't sleep. They stay up
walking on the roof. They're wildly awake.
They can't be tied down.

Love and a respectable hesitation
don't mix. It's time to strip,
and quit being bashful.

Beloved, take our self-restraint
and strangle it.

Burn our houses. A lover's house
is better burnt! A candle gets more pointed
and brighter as it burns. Stay up
this one night. Walk the sleepless
precincts. Be with those
being killed in union.

Watch the ship of those creatures sink.
Go with Fariddin Attar as he takes his trays
of perfumes to the river and dumps them in.

Walk into the river,
and then walk out.

How long do you plan to stay in your ecstasy,
where all you can say is, "I don't know *anything*?"

Let your *I don't see* become *I see*.
Move beyond the excitement,
and your *ideas* of surrendering.

There are hundreds of love-drunkards
walking the street. Wake into the sobriety
that says, "I am sustained from within."

(*Mathnawi*, VI, 576-631)

The Open Window

God is the Lord,
who gave such beauty to Joseph
that his face like lakewater
with white clouds in it
bloomed with light.

Joseph and Moses received God's light,
Joseph the light of beauty,
Moses the light of knowing.

In the midnight of this world,
Moses could see everything.

His face shot forth such a powerful beam
that he asked God for a veil,
so that others would not be blinded,
as adders are said to be
by the glint of an emerald.

He asked God for a feedbag
to fit over his face!

"Make one out of your felt robe.
That fabric is used to being permeated
with our light. It can stand the intensity."

The bodies of holy men and women have the ability
to endure the unconditional light
that can tear mountain ranges to pieces.

In a lamp niche there is a glass lamp,
and in that there is a light,
which nothing can hold.

Muhammed related that God said, "I am not in
the atmosphere, or in the void of space,
or in the most brilliant intelligences.
I live more clearly and brightly
as a guest in a humble worker's heart.

There I am, without qualification, or
definition, or description. I am there,
in that person's loving, so that my qualities
and powers can flow out into everything else.

In such a mirror, time and matter
can bear my beauty. Such a person is
a vast mirror, within which, every *second*,
fifty wedding banquets appear!

Don't ask me to describe it!"

The gist of this is that Moses could make a veil
because he knew God's penetrating power well.

His covering was a glory,
as a devoted person's face glows
with the guest, as a mystic
in ecstasy shines.

Fire can be stirred from embers,
because the embers already *know* the fire.

Safura, Moses' wife and the daughter of Shu'ayb,
loved God's light and the true guidance so much
that she sacrificed her eyesight.

She closed one eye and beheld the uncovered light
of Moses with the other. That eye was lost.
Then, she couldn't help herself!

She opened the other eye and spent it too.
Just as a spiritual warrior at first will give away
loaves of bread, and then his life.

Safura began to weep. "Are you grieving,"
asked a woman friend, "because you've lost
the beautiful jonquils of your eyes?"

"No, I'm crying that I don't have
a thousand more eyes to lavish on Moses.

My windows have been demolished by the moon,
but this ruin has no regrets, no memory even
of what the porch looked like, or the roof."

The light of Joseph's face, when he passed by a house,
would filter through the lattice and make a radiance
on the wall. People would notice and say,
"Joseph must be taking a walk."

It's fortunate to have a window that faces
that way! Open it up and stay in the opening,
so you can have more delight in Joseph.

The work of love is to open that window
in the chest and to look incessantly
on the Beloved. You can do this.

Listen. Make a way for yourself
inside your self. Stop looking
in the other way of looking.

You already have the precious mixture
that will make you well. Use it.

Old enemies will become friends.
Your beauty will be God's beauty.

Your friendlessness will change to moisture
and nourishment for your friends.

It's not a kingdom like any you know,
the kingdom of God that's within you,
but hundreds of thousands of kingdoms.

God gave Joseph the kingdom of beauty
and the kingdom of dream interpretation.
He didn't have to be taught that science.

The kingdom of physical beauty led him to jail:
the episode with Potiphar's wife.

But the kingdom of dream interpretation
gave him power greater than Pharoah's,
a stately mystery and depth like
Saturn with its rings.

(*Mathnawi*, VI, 3055-3105)

Why the Prophets Are Human

A woman came to Ali, "My baby has crawled out
on the roof near the water drain, where I cannot go.
He won't listen to me. I talk to him,
but he doesn't understand language.

I make gestures. I show him my breast,
but he turns away. What can I do?"

"Take another baby his age
up to the roof."

The woman did so, and her child saw his friend
and crawled away from the edge.

The prophets are human for this reason,
that we may see them and delight
in the friendly presence
and crawl away from the downspout.

(*Mathnawi*, IV, 2657-2669)

Ali in Battle

Learn from Ali how to fight
without your ego participating.

God's Lion did nothing
that didn't originate
from his deep center.

Once in battle he got the best of a certain knight
and quickly drew his sword. The man,
helpless on the ground, spat
in Ali's face. Ali dropped his sword,
relaxed, and helped the man to his feet.

"Why have you spared me?
How has lightning contracted back
into its cloud? Speak, my prince,
so that my soul can begin to stir
 in me like an embryo."

Ali was quiet and then finally answered,
"I am God's Lion, not the lion of passion.
The sun is my lord. I have no longing
except for the One.

When a wind of personal reaction comes,
I do not go along with it.

There are many winds full of anger,
and lust, and greed. They move the rubbish
around, but the solid mountain of our true nature
stays where it's always been.

There's nothing now
except the divine qualities.
Come through the opening into me.

Your impudence was better than any reverence,
because in this moment I am you and you are me.

I give you this opened heart as God gives gifts:
The poison of your spit has become
the honey of friendship."

(*Mathnawi*, I, 3721-3750,3764-3771,3773-3782,3787-
3789,3796-3798,3825-3830,3832,3841,3844)

The Witness, the Darling

Muhammed could mediate
for every kind of disgrace,
because he looked so unswervingly
at God. His eye-medicine came
from his ever-expanding into God.

Any orphan daubed with that salve
will get better. He could see all
the attainments of those on the way.

Hence God called him "The Witness."

The tools of The Witness are truthfulness
and keen seeing and the night vigil.

This is the witness a judge listens
most carefully to. A false witness
has some self-interest that makes
his testimony specious.

He can't see the whole. That's why God
wants you to deny your desires, so
you will learn how to give up self-interest.

It's the love of the manifest world
that makes you an unreliable witness.

There is another way of seeing
that sees *through* your love of this place,
through the exciting drunkenness to the headache.
The Witness can cure that hurting.

God is the just judge,
who calls the true Witness,
the eye of pure love,
the darling,
        the dalliance,
the reason inside the playfulness
that created phenomena.

(*Mathnawi*, VI, 2861-2883)

Notes

"Introduction"

Shams ~ Rumi's teacher. In the mysterious exchange that occurred between Rumi and Shams, the designations of student and teacher dissolved. Both were sheikh and disciple with each other. I have seen a reference to Shams' teacher being Najm al-Din Kubra, who died in 1221, but surely the friendship of Shams and Rumi transcended all former connections. That friendship became one of the great glories of mysticism.

There's not much to report about Shams. He has no life history. He lived in the true mystic's state, and his real work was done there, so that the external details are few. Annemarie Schimmel gives the most reliable account of the "facts" in *The Triumphal Sun,* but perhaps the legends in Aflaki's fourteenth century hagiography transmit better the essence of Shams:

> During his second exile from Rumi, in Damascus, Shams was frequently overwhelmed by the divine presence. When he felt that he could no longer endure the beauty, he would join some project with common laborers. He would continue to work far into the night. When it was time to be paid, he made some excuse. "Save it up for me. I have a debt that I want to repay." He never took wages for these times. Then he would go back to being lost in the ecstasy and in the longing for companionship. "Among the intimate friends of God is there no one to bear this with me?" A voice came from the world of mystery. "Among those who exist, Jelaluddin Rumi is your one friend."

> One day, during this second exile, Rumi called for his son, Sultan Veled, and told him, "Go to Damascus to the caravanserai on Salihiyye Mountain. There you'll find Shams playing dice with a young Frenchman. As they

finish, Shams will gather up the young man's money. He will strike Shams. Pay no attention to that. Throw these two thousand coins that I give you at Shams' feet, and let the entire company bow to him. The young Frank is a great teacher, although he doesn't know it yet. This companionship with Shams will help him to flower into perfection." Sultan Veled set out with twenty meditative friends, and when they arrived at the caravanserai, it was just as Rumi had said. The young man turned pale, fearing that he had offended someone of great spiritual magnificence. He took off his cap and offered all of his money to Shams. "No. Take it with you to Europe. Be the leader of that gathering of friends, and remember us in your prayers."

This "young Frenchman" is said to have been Francis of Assisi. All traditions connect at the core.

"The Gazelle"

Abu Bakr ~ (d. 634) The first Caliph of Islam. He held the Islamic community together after Muhammed's death. He is known as "Siddiq" (the faithful), and as the closest personal friend of the Prophet. His daughter Aisha, was Muhammed's favorite wife. The *Qur'an* makes reference to only two of the Prophet's contemporaries, Abu Bakr and the blind man who urgently interrupted Muhammed. Abu Bakr and Ali, are considered to be the two through whom the esoteric doctrines, known as *Tasawwuf*, were transmitted.

Qutb ~ means "axis," "pole," the "center" which contains the periphery, or is present in it. The Qutb is a spiritual reality, or function, which can reside in a human being, or several human beings, or a moment. It is the elusive mystery of how reality gets delegated into the manifest world, and obviously cannot be defined in a footnote, or held in language at all.

Husam Chelebi ~ Husam was Rumi's scribe. He succeeded Rumi as sheikh of the dervish learning community in Konya, Turkey.

The Georgia mountains ~ Rumi actually says "Abkhaz," which Nicholson explains in his note as "a mountainous region in Georgia" (in the Caucasus), a symbol of the "wilds," the confusion of this world--which, if the mystery were revealed, says Rumi–could become a Baghdad (which means "the gift of the Magi"), a place of illumination.

"The Earthquake That Frees Prisoners"

Bayazid Bestami ~ (d. 874) Born in Bistam in northern Iran. His tomb is there. He was the first of the "drunken sufis" who spoke of being naughted into union with God so that he could rephrase the customary prayer, *Subhan Allah,* "Glory to God," to "how great is my glory!"

> For thirty years, God was my mirror, but now I am my own mirror. That which used to be I, I am no more. To say "I" and "God" denies the Unity of God. I say I am my own mirror, but it is God who speaks with my tongue. I have vanished. I glided out of Bayazid-hood as a snake glides from a castoff skin. And then I looked and saw that lover and Beloved and love are ONE.
>
> *Encyclopedia of Islam*, ed. Gibb, Kramer, et al.

Azar ~ Azar was Abraham's father and a famous image-maker. In the *Qur'an* Abraham asks his father, *Do you take idols for gods?*

Azrael ~ The angel who separates the soul from the body at death.

> Azrael in Arabic tradition, was one of four angels (the others being Michael, Gabriel, and Israfel) sent to bring

back a handful of earth for the creation of Adam. Only
Azrael succeeded, and because of this he was given the
responsibility for separating body and soul; hence he is
known as the angel of death.

Gustav Davidson, *A Dictionary of Angels*

"The Berry of Relishing"

Shu'ayb ~ Shu'ayb is mentioned in the *Qur'an* as one of four
prophets sent specifically to the Arabs, along with Salih, Hud,
and Muhammed. He is also known as Jethro, the father-in-law
of Moses.

"Let That Laughter Lead You"

The Gospel that predicted Muhammed ~ There is a legend that
some early Christians found Muhammed's prophethood fore-
shadowed in a gospel together with his inward and outward
qualities, and that they were blessed by that devotion. Muham-
med's theory was that all revelation derived from one spiri-
tual "book" and therefore had a single essential identity. In
other words, the *Qur'an*, the *Gospels*, the *Old Testament*–all
sacred texts–come from an original.

"The Flap of the Wallet"

Omar ~ (d. 644) The second Caliph, designated as such by Abu
Bakr on his deathbed. Omar is famous for his strong will and
his direct, impetuous character. He formed the Islamic state
and expanded it into Syria, Iraq, Egypt, and Libya. Jerusalem
was also conquered during his reign.

> "Am I a king or a Caliph?" Omar once asked Salman the
> Persian. "If you tax the land of believers and put the
> money to any use the law allows, then you are a king and
> not a Caliph of Muhammed."

"By God!" said Omar, "I don't *know* whether I'm a king
or a Caliph. If I am a king, it's a fearful thing to be!"
                                    Concise Encyclopedia of Islam, ed. Cyril Glasse

Rum ~ "Rome," a designation for the section of Anatolia, the
western half, that was formerly a part of the Roman Empire.
This is the source of Rumi's name. "The one from Roman
Anatolia." In dialectical Arabic to this day, the adjective *rumi*
refers to that which is Western or non-indigenous.

"Neglecting Meditation and Refusing Kindnesses"

Saba ~ One of the kingdoms of southern Arabia, known in the
Bible as *Sheba*.

Gabriel ~ Gabriel ("God is my strength") is the angel of annun-
ciation, resurrection, mercy, vengeance, death, and revela-
tion. Muhammed claimed that it was Gabriel who dictated the
Qur'an to him.

"The Two-Way Pull of Freewill and the Freedom of the Involuntary Ball"

Khidr ~ literally, "the green one." Khidr is known through-
out the Islamic world. He exists on the edge between the seen
and the unseen. When Moses vows to find the place "where
the two seas meet," meaning where the spiritual and the
worldly mix, he meets Khidr. Although he's not mentioned by
name in the *Qur'an*, Khidr is associated with the persona
described as "one of our servants whom We [God] had given
mercy from Us, and We had taught him knowledge proceed-
ing from Us" (*Qur'an* 18:64, Arberry translation).

In this passage, Moses wants to follow Khidr and learn
from him, but Khidr says, "If you follow me, you must not
question anything I do. You must be patient and wait for my

explanations." Moses agrees, but as Khidr performs apparent outrages (sinking a boat, killing a boy), Moses cannot restrain his alarm, and Khidr leaves him after explaining the hidden reasons for his actions. Khidr represents the inner dimension which transcends form. He is the personification of the revealing function of the metaphysical intellect, the "prophetic soul." He especially appears to solitaries, those who are cut off from normal channels of spiritual instruction. The sufi mystic, Ibrahim (see "A New Life" and the note below), who gave up his external kingdom for the kingdom within, said this of Khidr:

> I lived four years in the wilderness. Khidr the Green
> Ancient was my companion. He taught me the Great
> Name of God.
>
> *Concise Encyclopedia of Islam*, ed. Cyril Glasse

Khidr is connected philologically with Elijah and with Utnapishtim of the Gilgamesh epic. He may be a partial source, along with Druidic lore, for the enigmatic Green Knight in the lovely Middle English poem, *Sir Gawain and the Green Knight*.

"A New Life"

Ibrahim ~ (d. 783) A Prince of Balkh, Ibrahim is a type to the sufis of someone who gives up, in one visionary moment, his external kingdom for the inner majesty. There are striking similarities between his life and Gautama the Buddha's. Balkh seems to have been an area where Buddhism, Islam, and Christianity met and blended. There are lotus motifs on the ancient ruins there. Here are several versions of Ibrahim's epiphany. Rumi's account is from the *Discourses*:

> Ibrahim, when he was still King, went out hunting. He
> galloped after a deer. He became completely separated
> from his retinue. His horse was tired and lathered, but

still Ibrahim rode. Deep in the wilderness, the fleeing
deer turned its head and spoke, "You were not created
for this chase. This deer body did not take shape out
of nothingness, so that you might hunt. Supposing you
catch me, will that be enough?" Ibrahim heard these
words deeply and cried out. He reined in his horse and
dismounted. There was a shepherd nearby. "Take this
royal jacket sewn with jewels. Take my horse and my
bow. Give me your shepherd's robe of coarse cloth, and
tell no one what has happened!" The exchange was made,
and Ibrahim set out on his new life. He made such an
extraordinary effort to catch the deer and ended up being
caught by God! All plans are subject to revision. God lives
between a human being and the object of his of her desire.
It's all a mystical journey to the Friend.

Discourse #44

Here is another account:

Ibrahim, son of Adham, was born of a princely family of
Balkh. One day he told, "I was seated on my seat of state,
and a mirror was offered for my self-inspection. I looked
in it. I saw only a wayfarer toward the tomb, bound for a
place where there would be no friend to cheer me. I saw
a long journey for which I had made no provision. I saw
a just judge, and myself unprovided with any proof for
my ordeal. My royalty became distasteful in that mo-
ment."

Concise Encyclopedia of Islam, ed. Cyril Glasse

Ibrahim turned at first to a Christian monk, Simeon, to
teach him the *ma'rifah* (mystical knowledge), and he later
found sufi masters. Of this way he said,

This is the sign of the knower, that his thoughts are mostly
engaged in meditation, and his words are mostly praise
and glorification of God, and his deeds are mostly of

devotion, and his eye is mostly fixed on the subtleties of
divine action and power.

ibid.

"Arrangements To Meet"

We are a deer ~ Others have also described the absorption of
disciple into teacher in terms of predator and prey. Meher
Baba: "My lovers may be likened to one who is fond of lions
and admires them so much that he keeps a lion in his own
home, but being afraid of the lion, he puts him in a cage. He
feeds the pet animal from a distance. There is love. There is
a desire to see Baba comfortable and happy, but all this is done,
keeping Baba segregated from one's own Self. What is wanted
is that the lovers should open the 'cage,' and through intense
love, throw themselves inside to become food for the Lion of
Love. The lover should permit himself to be totally consumed
through his own love for the Beloved"(C.B. Purdom, *The God
Man*).

Fariddin Attar ~ (1119-1230) Attar is the great perfumist and
physician-poet, author of *The Conference of the Birds*. He is said
to have met Rumi in Damascus when Rumi was a boy of
twelve traveling with his father. Attar immediately recog-
nized Rumi's spiritual eminence. He saw the father walking
ahead of the son and said,"Here comes a sea followed by an
ocean." He gave the boy his *Asranama*, a book about the entan-
glement of the soul in the material world.

"Why the Prophets Are Human"

Ali ~ (598-661) Muhammed's cousin, also his son-in-law, and
the Fourth Caliph. Ali's tomb is in Najaf, Iraq. He was one of
the first converts to Islam. Ali's relationship with Muhammed
was a special one. Twice he's referred to as "my brother" and
three times as "my heir." Muhammed blessed the marriage of
his daughter Fatima and Ali by anointing them on their

wedding night. Anointing is not a feature of Islamic ritual, and as far as is known, Muhammed did this for no one else. Ali is recognized by sufi mystics as a fountainhead of the esoteric secrets and more generally he is remembered as a model of *futuwwah* (or chivalry) as a great warrior, and for his learning. It was Ali who first laid down the rules of formal Arabic grammar, notably describing language as made up of nouns, verbs, and particles. The sayings and sermons of Ali are collected in *The Way of Eloquence,* which serves as a model for Arabic usage--much as the orations of Cicero did, until very recently, in the West.